~POCKET~
IRISH
POETRY

&
GILL &
MACMILLAN

Gill & Macmillan
Hume Avenue, Park West, Dublin 12

www.gillmacmillanbooks.ie

Copyright © Teapot Press Ltd 2015

ISBN 9780717166978

This book was created and produced by Teapot Press Ltd

Introduction and biographies by Fiona Biggs
Edited by Fiona Biggs
Designed by Tony Potter

Printed in PRC

This book is typeset in Garamond.

5 4 3 2 1

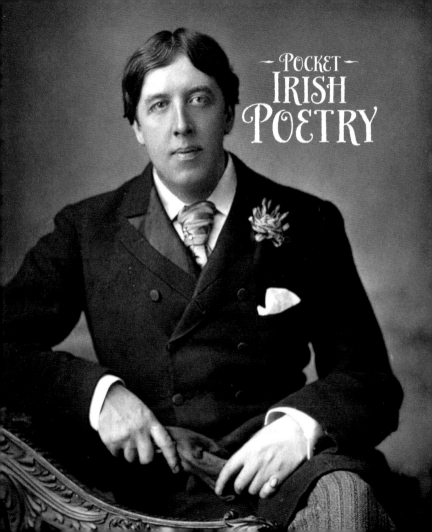

POCKET
IRISH
POETRY

Contents

INTRODUCTION

The Irish are a poetic race, in love with words and with the rhythms and music of language. It is no accident that many of the verses included here are song lyrics, whether they were written to be sung at gatherings or penned as poems that were later set to music. Ever since the days of the itinerant singers and storytellers who plied their art in exchange for bed and board, poetry and song have expressed the very soul of the nation, the hidden longings of its heart, its murmurings of love and its outpourings of grief, outrage and disillusion. This collection is by no means comprehensive – with such a vast body of work from which to choose, it could be said that we have barely skimmed the surface – but it dips into our collective consciousness in our times of happiness, dispossession, revolution, defeat and triumph. There are also, of course, the personal poems, telling of love rejected and requited, of maternal love and anguish and paternal age and frailty, of hopes dashed and ambitions achieved. Ireland's history is always reflected, indeed dissected by its poets, some of whose lives were violently cut short by insurrection and war, depriving the nation of their art and maturing insights.

Our poets come from all sides of the religious, political and class divide. Some are poets by profession; others are, variously, statesmen, orators, soldiers, playwrights and novelists, who have laid bare another side of themselves in their poetry. Here you will find poems by James Joyce, their light, gentle lyricism far removed from the boundary-pushing prose of his novels; Oscar Wilde's sparkling theatrical wit is unexpectedly absent from his plangent verses of love, longing and despair, seemingly written straight from the heart; Jonathan Swift's sharp and precisely targeted satirical pen trips lightly through his witty verses on life, on love. The political questions of the day are often dealt with obliquely, for example in James C. Mangan's 'Dark Rosaleen', one of many poems, known as 'aislings', in which Ireland is compared to a beautiful and distressed woman, or James McCarroll's strongly nationalist 'The Irish Wolf' – the title is a reference to a British characterization of the Irish people as wolves.

The Act of Union, 'this fetter vile', passed in 1801, effectively disempowered the Catholic population of Ireland, now in a minority in the United Kingdom of Great Britain and Ireland. Some of our greatest lyric poets were writing in the shadow of the passage of the Act, as were the many nationalist poets and activists produced by the ruling Protestant class, often regarded by later nationalist groups as unsympathetic to the Irish struggle for independence. Robert Emmet, executed for treason, was the youngest son of a wealthy Protestant family. His 'Arbour Hill' laments the fact that there is no monument to Ireland's fallen heroes – less than two hundred years later, Arbour Hill became the site of national remembrance. Lady Jane 'Speranza' Wilde's 'Lament for the Potato' is not the comic ditty that its title might suggest, but shows a deep awareness of the plight of a nation entirely dependent for sustenance on the failed potato crop. Thomas Davis' rallying cry 'A Nation Once Again' is an exploration of the distinct Irish identity, neither Catholic nor Protestant, in which he believed so strongly. W.B. Yeats, always an admirer of those idealists who sacrificed their lives for their country, pays more than lip service to Irish Protestant nationalists in his despairing and prophetic 'September 1913': 'Was it for this … that all that blood was shed, for this Edward Fitzgerald died, and Robert Emmet and Wolfe Tone, All that delirium of the brave?'

There is a lot of sentimentality between the covers of this small volume – to our modern sensibilities the poems may sometimes seem mawkish, or even trite. However, context, as always, is everything – much of the poetry presented here was written in the wake of defining events in the history of the people of Ireland. Great loss gives rise to outpourings of feeling that may seem excessive in our less turbulent times.

Poetry provides a unique perspective on the seismic events in the history of the nation. The story of Ireland has been a big one, and the poetry here reflects that long and eventful history, telling of a nation that has run the gamut from dispossession and rebellion to victory and independence. As a nation we have been viewed as constantly kicking over the traces; an unavoidable consequence of our centuries-long drive for independence and self-determination. However, several generations since that hard-won independence was gained, it might be said that we, as a people, have finally come of age – we have matured beyond the idealised image of ourselves that sustained us in times of hardship and despair, beyond the sometimes strutting confidence of a newly liberated nation, gradually coming to an acceptance of ourselves as we are, with all our human failings and idiosyncrasies. We can take time to stop and wonder at nature, to find the meaning in a work of art, and poets can turn their minds, hearts and pens to offering a perspective on the real issues of our lives today, those small details that preoccupy us as we make our way through daily life. Out of the crucible pours something pure and refined.

This 'most distressful country' has produced four Nobel laureates in the field of literature, including W.B. Yeats and Seamus Heaney, who have provided a sometimes uncomfortable commentary on the nation's tribulations. Charting our long journey from disempowerment and distress to independence and isolationism and on to prosperity, economic crisis and recovery, our poets, more than anyone, have allowed us to take our place in the world with pride.

Dónal Óg

It is late last night the dog was speaking of you;
the snipe was speaking of you in her deep marsh.
It is you are the lonely bird through the woods;
and that you may be without a mate until you find me.

You promised me, and you said a lie to me,
that you would be before me where the sheep are
  flocked;
I gave a whistle and three hundred cries to you,
and I found nothing there but a bleating lamb.

You promised me a thing that was hard for you,
a ship of gold under a silver mast;
twelve towns with a market in all of them,
and a fine white court by the side of the sea.

– Dónal Óg –

You promised me a thing that is not possible,
that you would give me gloves of the skin of a fish;
that you would give me shoes of the skin of a bird;
and a suit of the dearest silk in Ireland.

When I go by myself to the Well of Loneliness,
I sit down and I go through my trouble;
when I see the world and do not see my boy,
he that has an amber shade in his hair.

It was on that Sunday I gave my love to you;
the Sunday that is last before Easter Sunday
and myself on my knees reading the Passion;
and my two eyes giving love to you for ever.

My mother has said to me not to be talking with
   you today,
or tomorrow, or on the Sunday;
it was a bad time she took for telling me that;
it was shutting the door after the house was robbed.

My heart is as black as the blackness of the sloe,
or as the black coal that is on the smith's forge;
or as the sole of a shoe left in white halls;
it was you put that darkness over my life.

You have taken the east from me, you have taken the
    west from me;
you have taken what is before me and what is
    behind me;
you have taken the moon, you have taken the sun
    from me;
and my fear is great that you have taken God from me!

8th-century poem, translated by Lady Gregory (1855–1932)

Woman, Graceful as the Swan

WOMAN, graceful as the swan,
Why should I expire
For the fire of any eye,
Slender waist or swan-like limb,
Is't for them that I should die?

The round breasts, the fresh skin,
Cheeks crimson, hair like silk to touch,
Indeed, indeed, I shall not die,
Please God, not I, for any such!

The golden locks, the forehead thin,
The quiet mien, the gracious ease,
The rounded heel, the languid tone,
Fools alone find death from these.

Thy sharp wit, thy perfect calm,
Thy thin palm like foam of the sea;
Thy white neck, thy blue eye,
I shall not die for thee.

Woman, graceful as the swan,
A wise man did rear me, too,
Little palm, white neck, bright eye,
I shall not die for you.

Anonymous (13th–17th centuries)
Translated by Douglas Hyde (1838–1945)

She Moved Through the Fair

My young love said to me, 'My brothers won't mind
And my parents won't slight you for your lack
    of kind.'
Then she stepped away from me, and this she did say,
'It will not be long, love, till our wedding day.'

She stepped away from me and she moved through
    the fair,
And fondly I watched her go here and go there,
Then she went her way homeward with one star
    awake,
As the swan in the evening moves over the lake.

The people were saying no two were e'er wed
But one had a sorrow that never was said,
And I smiled as she passed with her goods and
    her gear,
And that was the last that I saw of my dear.

I dreamt it last night that my young love came in
So softly she entered, her feet made no din;
She came close beside me, and this she did say:
'It will not be long, love, till our wedding day.'

Translated by Padraic Colum (1881–1972)

On Stella's Birth-Day, 1719

STELLA this Day is thirty four,
(We shan't dispute a Year or more)
However, Stella, be not troubled,
Although thy Size and Years are doubled,
Since first I saw Thee at Sixteen
The brightest Virgin on the Green,
So little is thy Form declin'd
Made up so largely in thy Mind.
Oh, would it please the gods to split
Thy beauty, size, and years, and wit;
No age could furnish out a pair
Of nymphs so graceful, wise, and fair;
With half the lustre of your eyes,
With half your wit, your years, and size.
And then, before it grew too late,
How should I beg of gentle Fate,
(That either nymph might have her swain)
To split my worship too in twain.

Jonathan Swift (1667–1745)

From On His Own Deafness

DEAF, giddy, odious to my friends,
Now all my consolation ends;
No more I hear my church's bell
Than if it rang out for my knell;
At thunder now no more I start
Than at the rumbling of a cart.
Nay, though I know you do not credit –
Although a thousand times I've said it:
A scold whom you might hear a mile hence
No more could reach me than her silence.

Jonathan Swift (1667–1745)

The Amazonian Gift

Is Courage in a Woman's Breast
Less pleasing than in Man?
And is a smiling Maid allowed
No weapon but a fan?

'Tis true, her Tongue, I've heard 'em say,
Is Woman's chief Defence;
And if you'll b'lieve me, gentle Youths,
I have no Aid from thence.

And some will say that sparkling Eyes
More dang'rous are than Swords;
But I ne'er point my Eyes to kill,
Nor put I trust in words.

Then, since the Arms that Women use,
Successless are in me,
I'll take the Pistol, Sword or Gun,
And thus equipped, live free.

The pattern of the Spartan Dame
I'll copy as I can;
To Man, degen'rate Man, I'll give
That simple thing, a Fan.

Dorothea Dubois (1728–1774)

If A Daughter You Have

IF a daughter you have, she's the plague of your life,
No peace shall you know, tho' you've buried your wife,
At twenty she mocks at the duty you taught her,
O, what a plague is an obstinate daughter.
Sighing and whining,
Dying and pining,
O, what a plague is an obstinate daughter.
When scarce in their teens, they have wit to perplex us,
With letters and lovers for ever they vex us,
While each still rejects the fair suitor you've brought her,
O, what a plague is an obstinate daughter.
Wrangling and jangling,
Flouting and pouting,
O, what a plague is an obstinate daughter.

Richard Brinsley Sheridan (1751–1816)

Arbour Hill

No rising column marks this spot,
Where many a victim lies;
But oh! the blood that here has streamed,
To heaven for justice cries.

It claims it on the oppressor's head,
Who joys in human woe,
Who drinks the tears by misery shed,
And mocks them as they flow.

It claims it on the callous judge,
Whose hands in blood are dyed,
Who arms injustice with the sword,
The balance throws aside.

It claims it for his ruined isle,
Her wretched children's grave;
Where withered Freedom droops her head,
And man exists – a slave.

O sacred justice! Free this land
From tyranny abhorred;
Resume thy balance and thy seat –
Resume – but sheathe thy sword.

No retribution should we seek –
Too long has horror reigned;
By mercy marked may freedom rise,
By cruelty unstained.

Nor shall the tyrant's ashes mix
With those our martyred dead;
This is the place where Erin's sons
In Erin's cause have bled.

And those who here are laid at rest,
Oh! Hallowed be each name;
Their memories are forever blest –
Consigned to endless fame.

Unconsecrated is this ground,
Unblest by holy hands;
No bell here tolls its solemn sound,
No monument here stands.

But here the patriot's tears are shed,
The poor man's blessing given;
They consecrate their virtuous dead,
These waft their fame to heaven.

Robert Emmet (1778–1803)

The Lily

How wither'd, perish'd, seems the form
Of yon obscure unsightly root!
Yet from the blight of wintry storm
It hides secure the precious fruit.

The careless eye can find no grace,
No beauty in the scaly folds,
Nor see within the dark embrace
What latent loveliness it holds.

Yet in that bulb, those sapless scales
The lily wraps her silver vest,
Till vernal suns and vernal gales
Shall kiss once more her fragrant breast.

Yes, hide beneath the mould'ring heap,
The undelighting slighted thing;
There in the cold earth buried deep,
In silence let it wait the spring.

- THE LILY -

Oh! many a stormy night shall close
In gloom upon the barren earth,
While still in undisturb'd repose,
Uninjur'd lies the future birth.

And ignorance, with sceptic eye,
Hope's patient smile shall wond'ring view;
Or mock her fond credulity,
As her soft tears the spot bedew;

Sweet smile of hope, delicious tear,
The sun, the show'r indeed shall come,
The promised verdant shoot appear,
And nature bid her blossoms bloom.

And thou, O virgin queen of spring,
Shalt from thy dark and lowly bed,
Bursting thy green sheath's silken string,
Unveil thy charms, and perfume shed;

Unfold thy robes of purest white,
Unsullied from their darksome grave,
And thy soft petals' flow'ry light,
In the mild breeze unfetter'd wave.

So faith shall seek the lowly dust,
Where humble sorrow loves to lie,
And bid her thus her hopes intrust,
And watch with patient, cheerful eye;

And bear the long, cold, wintry night,
And bear her own degraded doom,
And wait till heav'n's reviving light,
Eternal spring! shall burst the gloom.

Mary Tighe (1772–1810)

My Father

Who took me from my mother's arms,
And, smiling at her soft alarms,
Showed me the world and Nature's charms?

Who made me feel and understand
The wonders of the sea and land,
And mark, through all, the Maker's hand?

Who climbed with me the mountain's height,
And watched my look of dread delight,
While rose the glorious orb of light?

Who from each flower and verdant stalk
Gathered a honey'd store of talk,
And fill'd the long, delightful walk?

Not on an insect would he tread,
Nor strike the stinging-nettle dead –
Who taught, at once, my heart and head?

Who fired my breast with Homer's fame,
And taught the high heroic theme
That nightly flashed upon my dream?

Who smiled at my supreme desire
To see the curling smoke aspire
From Ithaca's domestic fire?

Who, with Ulysses, saw me roam,
High on the raft, amidst the foam,
His head upraised to look for home?

'What made a barren rock so dear?'
'My boy, he had a country there!'
And who, then, dropped a precious tear?

Who now, in pale and placid light
Of memory, gleams upon my sight,
Bursting the sepulchre of night?

O! teach me still thy Christian plan,
For practice with thy precept ran,
Nor yet desert me, now a man.

Still let thy scholar's heart rejoice
With charm of thy angelic voice;
Still prompt the motive and the choice –

For yet remains a little space,
Till I shall meet thee face to face,
And not, as now, in vain embrace –
MY FATHER!

William Drennan (1754–1820)

Dark Rosaleen

O MY Dark Rosaleen,
Do not sigh, do not weep!
The priests are on the ocean green,
They march along the deep.
There's wine…from the royal Pope,
Upon the ocean green;
And Spanish ale shall give you hope,
My Dark Rosaleen!
My own Rosaleen!
Shall glad your heart, shall give you hope,
Shall give you health, and help, and hope,
My Dark Rosaleen!

Over hills, and through dales,
Have I roamed for your sake;
All yesterday I sailed with sails
On river and on lake.
The Erne…at its highest flood,
I dashed across unseen,

For there was lightning in my blood,
Red lightning lightened through my blood,
My Dark Rosaleen!

All day long, in unrest,
To and fro, do I move.
The very soul within my breast
Is wasted for you, love!
The heart...in my bosom faints
To think of you, my Queen,
My life of life, my saint of saints,
My Dark Rosaleen!
My own Rosaleen!
To hear your sweet and sad complaints,
My life, my love, my saint of saints,
My Dark Rosaleen!
Woe and pain, pain and woe,
Are my lot, night and noon,
To see your bright face clouded so,

Like to the mournful moon.
But yet...will I rear your throne
Again in golden sheen;
'Tis you shall reign, and reign alone,
My Dark Rosaleen!

Over dews, over sands,
Will I fly, for your weal;
Your holy delicate white hands
Shall girdle me with steel.
At home...in your emerald bowers,
From morning's dawn till e'en,
You'll pray for me, my flower of flowers,
My Dark Rosaleen!

I could scale the blue air,
I could plough the high hills,
Oh, I could kneel all night in prayer,
To heal your many ills!

And one…beamy smile from you
Would float like light between
My toils and me, my own, my true,
My Dark Rosaleen!
My fond Rosaleen!
Would give me life and soul anew,
A second life, a soul anew,
My Dark Rosaleen!

O! the Erne shall run red
With redundance of blood,
The earth shall rock beneath our tread,
And flames wrap hill and wood,
And gun-peal, and slogan cry,
Wake many a glen serene,
Ere you shall fade, ere you shall die,
My Dark Rosaleen!

My own Rosaleen!
The Judgement Hour must first be nigh,
Ere you can fade, ere you can die,
My Dark Rosaleen!

James Clarence Mangan (1803–1849)

Rest Only in the Grave

I RODE till I reached the House of Wealth
'Twas filled with riot and blighted health.

I rode till I reached the House of Love –
'Twas vocal with sighs beneath and above!

I rode till I reached the House of Sin –
There were shrieks and curses without and within.

I rode till I reached the House of Toil –
Its inmates had nothing to bake or boil.

I rode in search of the House of Content
But never could reach it, far as I went!
The House of Quiet, for strong and weak
And poor and rich, I have still to seek –

That House is narrow, and dark, and small –
But the only Peaceful House of all.

James Clarence Mangan (1803–1849)

The Harp That Once Through Tara's Halls

THE harp that once through Tara's halls
The soul of music shed,
Now stands as mute on Tara's walls
As if that soul were fled.
So sleeps the pride of former days,
So glory's thrill is o'er
And hearts, that once beat high for praise,
Now feel that pulse no more.

No more to chiefs and ladies bright
The harp of Tara swells;
The chord alone, that breaks at night,
Its tale of ruin tells.
Thus Freedom now so seldom wakes,
The only throb she gives,
Is when some heart indignant breaks,
To show that she still lives.

Thomas Moore (1779–1852)

As Slow Our Ship

As slow our ship her foamy track
Against the wind was cleaving,
Her trembling pennant still look'd back
To that dear isle 'twas leaving.

So loath we part from all we love,
From all the links that bind us;
So turn our hearts as on we rove,
To those we've left behind us.

When, round the bowl, of vanish'd years
We talk, with joyous seeming, –
With smiles that might as well be tears,
So faint, so sad their beaming;

While memory brings us back again
Each early tie that twined us,
Oh, sweet's the cup that circles then
To those we've left behind us.

And when, in other climes, we meet
Some isle, or vale enchanting,
Where all looks flowery, wild, and sweet,
And nought but love is wanting;

We think how great had been our bliss,
If Heaven had but assign'd us
To live and die in scenes like this,
With some we've left behind us!

As travellers oft look back at eve,
When eastward darkly going,
To gaze upon that light they leave
Still faint behind them glowing –

So, when the close of pleasure's day
To gloom hath near consign'd us,
We turn to catch one fading ray
Of joy that's left behind us.

Thomas Moore (1779–1852)

The Meeting of the Waters

THERE is not in the wide world a valley so sweet
As that vale in whose bosom the bright waters meet;
Oh! the last rays of feeling and life must depart,
Ere the bloom of that valley shall fade from my heart.

Yet it was not that nature had shed o'er the scene
Her purest of crystal and brightest of green;
'Twas not her soft magic of streamlet or hill,
Oh! no, – it was something more exquisite still.

'Twas that friends, the beloved of my bosom, were near,
Who made every dear scene of enchantment more dear,
And who felt how the best charms of nature improve,
When we see them reflected from looks that we love.

Sweet vale of Avoca, how calm could I rest
In thy bosom of shade, with the friends I love best,
Where the storms that we feel in this cold world should
    cease,
And our hearts, like thy waters, be mingled in peace.

Thomas Moore (1779–1852)

An Argument

I've oft been told by learned friars,
That wishing and the crime are one,
And Heaven punishes desires
As much as if the deed were done.

If wishing damns us, you and I
Are damned to all our heart's content;
Come, then, at least we may enjoy
Some pleasure for our punishment!

Thomas Moore (1779–1852)

'Tis the Last Rose of Summer

'Tis the last rose of summer,
Left blooming alone;
All her lovely companions
Are faded and gone;
No flower of her kindred,
No rose-bud is nigh,
To reflect back her blushes,
Or give sigh for sigh!

I'll not leave thee, thou lone one!
To pine on the stem;
Since the lovely are sleeping,
Go, sleep thou with them;
Thus kindly I scatter
Thy leaves o'er the bed,
Where thy mates of the garden
Lie scentless and dead.

So soon may I follow,
When friendships decay,
And from love's shining circle
The gems drop away!
When true hearts lie wither'd,
And fond ones are flown,
Oh! Who would inhabit
This bleak world alone?

Thomas Moore (1779–1852)

O'Connell's Statue

CHISEL the likeness of The Chief,
Not in gaiety, nor grief;
Change not by your art to stone,
Ireland's laugh, or Ireland's moan.
Dark her tale, and none can tell
Its fearful chronicle so well.
Her frame is bent – her wounds are deep –
Who, like him, her woes can weep?
He can be gentle as a bride,
While none can rule with kinglier pride;
Calm to hear, and wise to prove,
Yet gay as lark in soaring love.

Well it were, posterity
Should have some image of his glee;
That easy humour, blossoming
Like the thousand flowers of spring!
Glorious the marble which could show
His bursting sympathy for woe:

Could catch the pathos, flowing wild,
Like mother's milk to craving child.

An oh! How princely were the art
Could mould his mien, or tell his heart
When sitting sole on Tara's hill,
While hung a million on his will!
Yet, not in gaiety nor grief,
Chisel the image of our Chief;
Nor even in that haughty hour
When a nation owned his power.

But would you by your art unroll
His own and Ireland's secret soul,
And give to other times to scan
The greatest greatness of the man?
Fierce defiance let him be
Hurling at our enemy –
From a base as fair and sure,

As love is true and pure,
Let his statue rise as tall
And firm as a castle wall;
On his broad brow let there be
A type of Ireland's history;
Pious, generous, deep, and warm,
Strong and changeful as a storm;
Let whole centuries of wrong,
Upon his recollection throng –
Strongbow's force, and Henry's wile,
Tudor's wrath, and Stuart's guile,
And iron Strafford's tiger jaws,
And brutal Brunswick's penal laws;
Not forgetting Saxon faith,
Not forgetting Norman scath,
Not forgetting William's word,
Not forgetting Cromwell's sword.
Let the Union's fetter vile –
The shame and ruin of our isle –

Let the blood of 'Ninety-Eight
And our present blighting fate –
Let the poor mechanic's lot,
And the peasant's ruined cot,
Plundered wealth and glory flown,
Ancient honours overthrown –
Let trampled altar, rifled urn,
Knit his look to purpose stern.
Mould all this into one thought,
Like wizard cloud with thunder fraught;
Still let our glories through it gleam,
Like fair flowers through a flooded stream,
Or like a flashing wave at night,
Bright, – 'mid the solemn darkness, bright.
Let the memory of old days
Shine through the statesman's anxious face –
Dathi's power, and Brian's fame,
And headlong Sarsfield's sword of flame;
And the spirit of Red Hugh,

And the pride of 'Eighty-Two,
And the victories he won,
And the hope that leads him on!

Let whole armies seem to fly
From his threatening hand and eye;
Be the strength of all the land
Like a falchion in his hand,
And be his gesture sternly grand.
A braggart tyrant swore to smite
A people struggling for their right;
O'Connell dared him to the field,
Content to die, but never yield.
Fancy such a soul as his,
In a moment such as this,
Like a cataract, or foaming tide,
Or army charging in its pride.
Thus he spoke, and thus he stood,
Proffering in our cause his blood.

Thus his country loves him best –
To image this is your behest.
Chisel thus, and thus alone,
If to man you'd change the stone.

Thomas Davis (1814–1845)

A Nation Once Again

WHEN boyhood's fire was in my blood
I read of ancient freemen
For Greece and Rome who bravely stood,
Three hundred men and three men.
And then I prayed I yet might see
Our fetters rent in twain,
And Ireland, long a province, be
A nation once again.

And, from that time, through wildest woe,
That hope has shone, a far light;
Nor could love's brightest summer glow
Outshine that solemn starlight:
It seemed to watch above my head
In forum, field and fane;
Its angel voice sang round my bed,
A nation once again.

It whispered, too, that freedom's ark
And service high and holy,
Would be profaned by feelings dark
And passions vain or lowly:
For freedom comes from God's right hand,
And needs a godly train;
And righteous men must make our land
A nation once again.

So, as I grew from boy to man,
I bent me to that bidding –
My spirit of each selfish plan
And cruel passion ridding;
For, thus I hoped some day to aid –
Oh! can such hope be vain? –
When my dear country shall be made
A nation once again.

Thomas Davis (1814–1845)

My Land

She is a rich and rare land;
Oh! She's a fresh and fair land;
She is a dear and rare land –
This native land of mine.

No men than hers are braver –
Her women's hearts ne'er waver;
I'd freely die to save her,
And think my lot divine.

She's not a dull or cold land;
No! She's a warm and bold land;
Oh! She's a true and old land –
This native land of mine.

Could beauty ever guard her,
And virtue still reward her,
No foe would cross her border –
No friend within it pine!

Oh! She's a fresh and fair land;
Oh! She's a true and rare land;
Yes! She's a rare and fair land –
This native land of mine.

Thomas Davis (1814–1845)

The West's Asleep

WHEN all beside a vigil keep,
The West's asleep, the West's asleep –
Alas! and well may Erin weep,
When Connaught lies in slumber deep.
There lake and plain smile fair and free,
'Mid rocks – their guardian chivalry –
Sing oh! let man learn liberty
From crashing wind and lashing sea.

That chainless wave and lovely land
Freedom and Nationhood demand –
Be sure, the great God never planned
For slumbering slaves, a home so grand.
And, long, a brave and haughty race
Honoured and sentinelled the place –
Sing oh! not even their sons' disgrace
Can quite destroy their glory's trace.

For often, in O'Connor's van,
To triumph dashed each Connaught clan –
And fleet as deer the Normans ran
Through Corlieu's Pass and Ardrahan.
And later times saw deeds as brave;
And glory guards Clanricarde's grave –
Sing oh! they died their land to save,
At Aughrim's slopes and Shannon's wave.

And if, when all a vigil keep,
The West's asleep, the West's asleep –
Alas! and well may Erin weep,
That Connaught lies in slumber deep.
But, hark! some voice like thunder spake:
'The West's awake! the West's awake!' –
'Sing oh! hurra! let England quake,
We'll watch till death for Erin's sake!'

Thomas Davis (1814–1845)

Lament for Thomas Davis

I WALKED through Ballinderry in the spring-time
When the bud was on the tree;
And I said, in every fresh-ploughed field beholding
The sowers striding free,
Scattering broadcast forth the corn in golden plenty
On the quick seed-clasping soil,
'Even such, this day, among the fresh-stirred hearts of Erin,
Thomas Davis, is thy toil!'

I sat by Ballyshannon in the summer,
And saw the salmon leap;
And I said, as I beheld the gallant creatures
Spring glittering from the deep,
Thro' the spray, and thro' the prone heaps striving onward
To the calm clear streams above,
'So sleekest thou thy native founts of freedom,
    Thomas Davis,
In the brightness of strength and love!'

I stood on Derrybawn in the autumn,
And I heard the eagle call,
With a clangorous cry of wrath and lamentation
That filled the wide mountain hall
O'er the bare deserted place of his plundered eyrie;
And I said, as he screamed and soared,
'So callest thou, thou wrathful-soaring Thomas Davis,
For a nation's rights restored!'

And, alas! To think but now, and thou art lying,
Dear Davis, dead at thy mother's knee;
And I, no mother near, on my own sick-bed,
That face on earth shall never see:
I may lie and try to feel that I am not dreaming,
I may lie and try to say, 'thy will be done' –
But a hundred such as I will never comfort Erin
For the loss of the noble son!

Young husbandman of Erin's fruitful seed-time,
In the fresh track of danger's plough!
Who will walk the heavy, toilsome, perilous furrow
Girt with freedom's seed-sheets now?
Who will banish with the wholesome crop of knowledge
The flaunting weed and the bitter thorn,
Now that thou thyself art but a seed for hopeful planting
Against the Resurrection morn?

Young salmon of the flood-tide of freedom
That swells round Erin's shore!
Thou wilt leap against their loud oppressive torrent
Of bigotry and hate no more:
Drawn downward by their prone material instinct,
Let them thunder on their rocks and foam –
Thou hast leapt, aspiring soul, to founts beyond
   their raging
Where troubled waters never come!

But I grieve not, eagle of the empty eyrie,
That thy wrathful cry is still;
And that the songs alone of peaceful mourners
Are heard today on Erin's hill;
Better far, if brother's war be destined for us
(God avert that horrid day, I pray),
That ere our hands be stained with slaughter fratricidal
Thy warm heart should be cold in clay.

But my trust is strong in God, who made us brothers,
That He will not suffer those right hands
Which thou hast joined in holier rites than wedlock
To draw opposing brands.
Oh, many a tuneful tongue that thou mad'st vocal
Would lie cold and silent then;
And songless long once more, should often-widowed
  Erin
Mourn the loss of her brave young men.

Oh, brave young men, my love, my pride, my promise,
'Tis on you my hopes are set,
In manliness, in kindliness, in justice,
To make Erin a nation yet:
Self-respecting, self-relying, self-advancing,
In union or in severance, free and strong –
And if God grant this, then, under God, to
   Thomas Davis
Let the greater praise belong.

Samuel Ferguson (1810–1886)

Another and another and another...

ANOTHER and another and another
And still another sunset and sunrise,
The same yet different, different yet the same,
Seen by me now in my declining years
As in my early childhood, youth and manhood;
And by my parents and my parents' parents,
And by the parents of my parents' parents,
And by their parents counted back for ever,
Seen, all their lives long, even as now by me;
And by my children and my children's children
And by the children of my children's children
And by their children counted on for ever

Still to be seen as even now seen by me;
Clear and bright sometimes, sometimes dark
   and clouded
But still the same sunsetting and sunrise;
The same for ever to the never ending
Line of observers, to the same observer
Through all the changes of his life the same:
Sunsetting and sunrising and sunsetting,
And then again sunrising and sunsetting,
Sunrising and sunsetting evermore.

James Henry (1798–1876)

Do You Remember That Night?

Do you remember that night
When you were at the window,
With neither hat nor gloves,
Nor coat to shelter you?
I reached out my hand to you
And you ardently grasped it,
I remained to converse with you
Until the lark began to sing.

Do you remember that night
That you and I were
At the foot of the rowan tree,
And the night drifting snow?
Your head on my breast,
And your pipe sweetly playing?
Little thought I that night
That our love ties would loosen!

The fire is unraked,
The light unextinguished,
The key under the door,
Do you softly draw it.
My mother is asleep,
And I am wide awake;
My fortune in my hand,
I am ready to go with you.

Beloved of my inmost heart,
Come some night, and soon,
When my people are at rest,
That we may talk together.
My arms shall encircle you,
While I relate my sad tale
That your soft, pleasant converse
Hath deprived me of heaven.

Eugene O'Curry (1794–1862)

The Irish Wolf

SEEK music in the wolf's fierce howl
Or pity in his bloodshot eye,
When hunger drives him out to prowl
Beneath a rayless northern sky:

But seek not that we should forgive
The hand that strikes us to the heart,
And yet in mockery bids us live
To count our stars as they depart.

We've fed the tyrant with our blood;
Won all his battles – built his throne –
Established him on land and flood,
And sought his glory next our own.

We raised him from his low estate;
We plucked his pagan soul from hell,
And led him pure to heaven's gate,
Till he, for gold, like Judas fell.

And when in one long, soulless night,
He lay unknown to wealth or fame,
We gave him empire – riches – light,
And taught him how to spell his name.

But now, ungenerous and unjust,
Forgetful of our old renown,
He bows us to the very dust;
But wears our jewels in his crown.

James McCarroll (1814–1892)

The Croppy Boy: A Ballad of '98

'GOOD men and true! in this house who dwell,
To a stranger *bouchal*, I pray you tell
Is the Priest at home? or may he be seen?
I would speak a word with Father Green.'

'The Priest's at home, boy, and may be seen;
'Tis easy speaking with Father Green;
But you must wait, till I go and see
If the holy Father alone may be.'

The youth has entered an empty hall –
What a lonely sound his light foot-fall!
And the gloomy chamber's chill and bare,
With a vested Priest in a lonely chair.

The youth has knelt to tell his sins.
'*Nomine Dei*,' the youth begins:
At '*mea culpa*' he beats his breast,
And in broken murmurs he speaks the rest.

'At the siege of Ross did my father fall,
And at Gorey my loving brothers all.
I alone am left of my name and race;
I will go to Wexford and take their place.

'I cursed three times since last Easter Day –
At Mass-time once I went to play;
I passed the churchyard one day in haste,
And forgot to pray for my mother's rest.

'I bear no hate against living thing;
But I love my country above my King.
Now, Father! bless me, and let me go
To die, if God has ordained it so.'

The Priest said nought, but a rustling noise
Made the youth look above in wild surprise;
The robes were off, and in scarlet there
Sat a yeoman captain with fiery glare.

With fiery glare and with fury hoarse,
Instead of blessing, he breathed a curse:
''Twas a good thought, boy, to come here
    and shrive;
For one short hour is your time to live.

'Upon yon river three tenders float:
The Priest's in one, if he isn't shot;
We hold his house for our Lord the King,
And – Amen, say I – may all traitors swing!'

At Geneva barrack that young man died,
And at Passage they have his body laid.
Good people who live in peace and joy,
Breathe a prayer and a tear for the Croppy Boy.

Carroll Malone (182?–1892)

A Lament for the Potato

THERE is woe, there is clamour, in our desolated land,
And wailing lamentation from a famine-stricken band;
And weeping are the multitudes in sorrow and despair,
For the green fields of Munster lying desolate and bare.
Woe for Lorc's ancient kingdom, sunk in slavery
    and grief;
Plundered, ruined, are our gentry, our people, and
    their Chief;

For the harvest lieth scattered, more worth to us
    than gold,
All the kindly food that nourished both the young and
    the old.
Well I mind me of the cosherings, where princes
    might dine,
And we drank until nightfall the best seven sorts of wine;
Yet was ever the Potato our old, familiar dish,
And the best of all sauces with the beeves and the fish.

But the harp now is silent, no one careth for the sound;
No flowers, no sweet honey, and no beauty can be found;
Not a bird its music trilling through the leaves of
   the wood,
Nought but weeping and hands wringing in despair for
   our food.

And the Heavens, all in darkness, seem lamenting
   our doom,
No brightness in the sunlight, not a ray to pierce
   the gloom;
The cataract comes rushing with a fearful deepened roar,
And ocean bursts its boundaries, dashing wildly on
   the shore.
Yet, in misery and want, we have one protecting man,
Kindly Barry, of Fitzstephen's old hospitable clan;
By mount and river working deeds of charity and grace:
Blessings ever on our champion, best hero of his race!
Save us, God! In Thy mercy bend to hear the people's cry,

From the famine-stricken fields, rising bitterly on high;
Let the mourning and the clamour cease in Lorc's
   ancient land,
And shield us in the death-hour by Thy strong,
   protecting hand!

Jane Wilde (1821–1896)

The Rock of Cashel

ROYAL and saintly Cashel! I would gaze
Upon the wreck of thy departed powers,
Not in the dewy light of matin hours,
Nor the meridian pomp of summer's blaze,
But at the close of dim autumnal days,
When the sun's parting glance, through slanting showers,
Sheds o'er thy rock-throned battlements and towers
Such awful gleams as brighten o'er Decay's
Prophetic cheek. At such a time, methinks,
There breathes from thy lone courts and voiceless aisles
A melancholy moral; such as sinks
On the lone traveller's heart, amid the piles
Of vast Persepolis on her mountain stand,
Or Thebes half buried in the desert sand.

Aubrey de Vere (1814–1902)

The Little Black Rose

THE little black rose shall be red at last;
What made it black but the March wind dry,
And the tear of the widow that fell on it fast?
It shall redden the hills when June is nigh!

The Silk of the Kine shall rest at last;
What drove her forth but the dragon fly?
In the golden vale she shall feed full fast,
With her mild gold horn and her slow, dark eye.

The wounded wood-dove lies dead at last!
The pine long-bleeding, it shall not die!
This song is secret. Mine ear it passed
In a wind o'er the plains at Athenry.

Aubrey de Vere (1814–1902)

A White Rose

THE red rose whispers of passion,
And the white rose breathes of love;
Oh, the red rose is a falcon,
And the white rose is a dove.

But I send you a cream-white rosebud
With a flush on its petal tips;
For the love that is purest and sweetest
Has a kiss of desire on the lips.

John Boyle O'Reilly (1844–1890)

A Passage

THE world was made when a man was born;
He must taste for himself the forbidden springs,
He can never take warning from old-fashioned things;
He must fight as a boy, he must drink as a youth,
He must kiss, he must love, he must swear to the truth
Of the friend of his soul, he must laugh to scorn the
   hint of deceit in a woman's eyes
That are clear as the wells of Paradise.
And so he goes on, till the world grows old,
Till his tongue has grown cautious, his heart has grown
   cold,
Till the smile leaves his mouth, and the ring leaves his
   laugh
And he shirks the bright headache you ask him to quaff;
He grows formal with men, and with women polite,
And distrustful of both when they're out of his sight;
Then he eats for his palate, and drinks for his head,
And loves for his pleasure, – and 'tis time he was dead!

John Boyle O'Reilly (1844–1890)

Le Jardin

THE lily's withered chalice falls
Around its rod of dusty gold,
And from the beech-trees on the wold
The last wood-pigeon coos and calls.

The gaudy leonine sunflower
Hangs black and barren on its stalk,
And down the windy garden walk
The dead leaves scatter, – hour by hour.

Pale privet-petals white as milk
Are blown into a snowy mass:
The roses lie upon the grass
Like little shreds of crimson silk.

Oscar Wilde (1854–1900)

Endymion

THE apple trees are hung with gold,
And birds are loud in Arcady,
The sheep lie bleating in the fold,
The wild goat runs across the wold,
But yesterday his love he told,
I know he will come back to me.
O rising moon! O Lady moon!
Be you my lover's sentinel,
You cannot choose but know him well,
For he is shod with purple shoon,
You cannot choose but know my love,
For he a shepherd's crook doth bear,
And he is soft as any dove,
And brown and curly is his hair.

The turtle now has ceased to call
Upon her crimson-footed groom,
The grey wolf prowls about the stall,
The lily's singing seneschal
Sleeps in the lily-bell, and all
The violet hills are lost in gloom.
O risen moon! O holy moon!
Stand on the top of Helice,
And if my own true love you see,
Ah! if you see the purple shoon,
The hazel crook, the lad's brown hair,
The goat-skin wrapped about his arm,
Tell him that I am waiting where
The rushlight glimmers in the Farm.

The falling dew is cold and chill,
And no bird sings in Arcady,
The little fauns have left the hill,
Even the tired daffodil
Has closed its gilded doors, and still
My lover comes not back to me.
False moon! False moon! O waning moon!
Where is my own true lover gone,
Where are the lips vermilion,
The shepherd's crook, the purple shoon?
Why spread that silver pavilion,
Why wear that veil of drifting mist?
Ah! thou hast young Endymion,
Thou hast the lips that should be kissed!

Oscar Wilde (1854–1900)

From The Ballad of Reading Gaol

HE did not wear his scarlet coat,
For blood and wine are red,
And blood and wine were on his hands
When they found him with the dead,
The poor dead woman whom he loved,
And murdered in her bed.

He walked amongst the Trial Men
In a suit of shabby grey;
A cricket cap was on his head,
And his step seemed light and gay;
But I never saw a man who looked
So wistfully at the day.

I never saw a man who looked
With such a wistful eye
Upon that little tent of blue
Which prisoners call the sky,
And at every drifting cloud that went

With sails of silver by.
I walked, with other souls in pain,
Within another ring,
And was wondering if the man had done
A great or little thing,
When a voice behind me whispered low,
'That fellow's got to swing.'

Dear Christ! The very prison walls
Suddenly seemed to reel,
And the sky above my head became
Like a casque of scorching steel;
And, though I was a soul in pain,
My pain I could not feel.

I only knew what hunted thought
Quickened his step, and why
He looked upon the garish day
With such a wistful eye;

The man had killed the thing he loved
And so he had to die.

Yet each man kills the thing he loves
By each let this be heard,
Some do it with a bitter look,
Some with a flattering word,
The coward does it with a kiss,
The brave man with a sword!

Some kill their love when they are young,
And some when they are old,
Some strangle with the hands of Lust,
Some with the hands of Gold…
The kindest use a knife because
The dead so soon grow cold.

Some love too little, some too long,
Some sell, and others buy;

Some do the deed with many tears,
And some without a sigh:
For each man kills the thing he loves,
Yet each man does not die.

He does not die a death of shame
On a day of dark disgrace,
Nor have a noose about his neck,
Nor a cloth upon his face,
Nor drop feet foremost through the floor
Into an empty space.

He does not sit with silent men
Who watch him night and day;
Who watch him when he tries to weep,
And when he tries to pray;
Who watch him lest himself should rob
The prison of its prey.

He does not wake at dawn to see
Dead figures throng his room,
The shivering Chaplain robed in white,
The Sheriff stern with gloom,
And the Governor all in shiny black,
With the yellow face of Doom.

Oscar Wilde (1854–1900)

On an Island

You've plucked a curlew, drawn a hen,
Washed the shirts of seven men,
You've stuffed my pillow, stretched the sheet,
And filled the pan to wash your feet,
You've cooped the pullets, wound the clock,
And rinsed the young men's drinking crock;
And now we'll dance to jigs and reels,
Nailed boots chasing girls' naked heels,
Until your father'll start to snore,
And Jude, now you're married, will stretch on the floor.

John Millington Synge (1871–1909)

In Kerry

WE heard the thrushes by the shore and sea,
And saw the golden stars' nativity,
Then round we went the lane by Thomas Flynn
Across the church where bones lie out and in;
And there I asked beneath a lonely cloud
Of strange delight, with one bird singing loud,
What change you'd wrought in graveyard, rock and sea,
This new wild paradise to wake for me . . .
Yet knew no more than knew these merry sins
Had built this stack of thigh-bones, jaws and shins.

John Millington Synge (1871–1909)

Prelude

STILL south I went and west and south again,
Through Wicklow from the morning till the night,
And far from cities, and the sights of men,
Lived with the sunshine, and the moon's delight.

I knew the stars, the flowers, and the birds,
The grey and wintry sides of many glens,
And did but half remember human words,
In converse with the mountains, moors, and fens.

John Millington Synge (1871–1909)

The Banshee

GREEN, in the wizard arms
Of the foam-bearded Atlantic,
An isle of old enchantment,
A melancholy isle,
Enchanted and dreaming lies;
And there, by Shannon's flowing,
In the moonlight, spectre-thin,
The spectre Erin sits.

An aged desolation,
She sits by old Shannon's flowing,
A mother of many children,
Of children exiled and dead,
In her home, with bent head, homeless,
Clasping her knees she sits,
Keening, keening!

And at her keen the fairy-grass
Trembles on dun and barrow;
Around the foot of her ancient crosses
The grave-grass shakes and the nettle swings;
In haunted glens the meadow-sweet
Flings to the night wind
Her mystic mournful perfume;
The sad spearmint by holy wells
Breathes melancholy balm.
Sometimes she lifts her head,
With blue eyes tearless,
And gazes athwart the reek of night
Upon things long past,
Upon things to come.

And sometimes, when the moon
Brings tempest upon the deep,
The roused Atlantic thunders from his caverns
    in the west,
The wolfhound at her feet
Springs up with a mighty bay,
And chords of mystery sound from the wild
    harp at her side,
Strung from the hearts of poets;
And she flies on the wings of tempest
With grey hair streaming:
A meteor of evil omen,
The spectre of hope forlorn,
Keening, keening!

She keens, and the strings of her wild
    harp shiver
On the gusts of night:
O'er the four waters she keens – over Moyle
    she keens,

O'er the Sea of Milith, and the Strait of
   Strongbow,
And the Ocean of Columbus.

And the Fianna hear, and the ghosts of her
   cloudy hovering heroes;
And the swan, Fianoula, wails o'er the waters of
   Inisfail,
Chanting her song of destiny,
The rune of weaving Fates.
And the nations hear in the void and quaking
   time of night,
Sad unto dawning, dirges,
Solemn dirges,
And snatches of bardic song;
Their souls quake in the void and quaking time
   of night,
And they dream of the weird of kings,

And tyrannies moulting, sick,
In the dreadful wind of change.

Wail no more, lonely one, mother of exiles, wail
  no more,
Banshee of the world – no more!
The sorrows are the world's, though art no
  more alone;
Thy wrongs, the world's.

John Todhunter (1839–1916)

The Dead at Clonmacnois

In a quiet water'd land, a land of roses,
Stands Saint Kieran's city fair;
And the warriors of Erin in their famous generations
Slumber there.

There beneath the dewy hillside sleep the noblest
Of the clan of Conn,
Each below his stone with name in branching Ogham
And the sacred knot thereon.

There they laid to rest the seven Kings of Tara,
There the sons of Cairbré sleep –
Battle-banners of the Gael, that in Kieran's plain
    of crosses
Now their final hosting keep.

And in Clonmacnois they laid the men of Teffia,
And right many a lord of Breagh;
Deep the sod above Clan Creidé and Clan Conaill,
Kind in hall and fierce in fray.

Many and many a son of Conn, the Hundred-Fighter,
In the red earth lies at rest;
Many a blue eye of Clan Colman the turf covers,
Many a swan-white breast.

T. W. Rolleston (1857–1920)

Autumnal

THE Autumn leaves are dying quietly,
Scarlet and orange, underfoot they lie;
They had their youth and prime
And now's the dying time;
Alas, alas, the young, the beloved, must die!

They are dying like the leaves of Autumn fast,
Scattered and broken, blown on every blast:
The darling young, the brave,
Love had no power to save.
Poor Love-lies-bleeding, Love's in ruins, downcast.

Alas, alas, the Autumn leaves are flying!
They had their Summer and 'tis time for dying.
But these had barely Spring.
Love trails a broken wing,
Walks through deserted woods, moaning and sighing.

Katharine Tynan (1861–1931)

Any Mother

'WHAT's the news? Now tell it me.'
'Allenby again advances.'
'No, it's not Allenby
But my boy, straight as a lance is.

'Oh, my boy it is that runs,
Hurls his young and slender body
On the dread death-dealing guns.
Oh, he's down! his head is bloody!'

'Haig's offensive has begun.'
'Say not Haig's nor any other,
Since it is my one sweet son
In the gases' risk and smother.

'He is taken by the throat,
In the bursting flame will quiver,
He the billet for all shot,
He the shell's objective ever.'

So not Allenby nor Haig,
But her darling goes to battle.
All the world's red mist and vague
Shattered by the scream and rattle.

Just one slender shape she sees,
One bright head tossed hither, thither;
Oh, if he goes down the seas
Whelm her and the world together!

Katharine Tynan (1861–1931)

The Wind that Shakes the Barley

THERE'S music in my heart all day,
I hear it late and early,
It comes from fields are far away,
The wind that shakes the barley.

Above the uplands drenched with dew
The sky hangs soft and pearly,
An emerald world is listening to
The wind that shakes the barley.

Above the bluest mountain crest
The lark is singing rarely,
It rocks the singer into rest,
The wind that shakes the barley.

Oh, still through summers and through springs
It calls me late and early.
Come home, come home, come home, it sings,
The wind that shakes the barley.

Katharine Tynan (1861–1931)

The Song of Wandering Aengus

I WENT out to the hazel wood,
Because a fire was in my head
And cut and peeled a hazel wand,
And hooked a berry to a thread;
And when white moths were on the wing,
And moth-like stars were flickering out,
I dropped the berry in a stream
And caught a little silver trout.

When I had laid it on the floor
I went to blow the fire aflame,
But something rustled on the floor,
And some one called me by my name:
It had become a glimmering girl
With apple blossom in her hair
Who called me by my name and ran
And faded through the brightening air.

Though I am old with wandering
Through hollow lands and hilly lands,
I will find out where she has gone,
And kiss her lips and take her hands;
And walk among long dappled grass,
And pluck till time and times are done
The silver apples of the moon,
The golden apples of the sun.

W. B. Yeats (1865–1939)

September 1913

WHAT need you, being come to sense,
But fumble in a greasy till
And add the halfpence to the pence
And prayer to shivering prayer, until

You have dried the marrow from the bone?
For men were born to pray and save:
Romantic Ireland's dead and gone,
It's with O'Leary in the grave.

Yet they were of a different kind,
The names that stilled your childish play,
They have gone about the world like wind,
But little time had they to pray

EXECUTION OF ROBERT EMMET,

IN THOMAS STREET 20ᵀᴴ SEPTEMBER 1803.

"MUST IRISHMEN LOOK IDLY ON, WHILE ENGLAND ASSASINATES AT WILL!"

For whom the hangman's rope was spun,
And what, God help us, could they save?
Romantic Ireland's dead and gone,
It's with O'Leary in the grave.

Was it for this the wild geese spread
The grey wing upon every tide;
For this that all that blood was shed,
For this Edward Fitzgerald died,

And Robert Emmet and Wolfe Tone,
All that delirium of the brave?
Romantic Ireland's dead and gone,
It's with O'Leary in the grave.

Yet could we turn the years again,
And call those exiles as they were
In all their loneliness and pain,
You'd cry, 'Some woman's yellow hair

Has maddened every mother's son':
They weighed so lightly what they gave.
But let them be, they're dead and gone,
They're with O'Leary in the grave.

W. B. Yeats (1865–1939)

Easter 1916

I HAVE met them at close of day
Coming with vivid faces
From counter or desk among grey
Eighteenth-century houses.
I have passed with a nod of the head
Or polite meaningless words,
Or have lingered awhile and said
Polite meaningless words,
And thought before I had done
Of a mocking tale or a gibe
To please a companion
Around the fire at the club,
Being certain that they and I
But lived where motley is worn:
All changed, changed utterly:
A terrible beauty is born.

That woman's days were spent
In ignorant good-will,

Her nights in argument
Until her voice grew shrill.
What voice more sweet than hers
When, young and beautiful,
She rode to harriers?
This man had kept a school
And rode our winged horse;
This other his helper and friend
Was coming into his force;
He might have won fame in the end,
So sensitive his nature seemed,
So daring and sweet his thought.
This other man I had dreamed
A drunken, vainglorious lout.
He had done most bitter wrong
To some who are near my heart,
Yet I number him in the song;
He, too, has resigned his part
In the casual comedy;

He, too, has been changed in his turn,
Transformed utterly;
A terrible beauty is born.

Hearts with one purpose alone
Through summer and winter seem
Enchanted to a stone
To trouble the living stream.
The horse that comes from the road,
The rider, the birds that range
From cloud to tumbling cloud,
Minute by minute they change;
A shadow of cloud on the stream
Changes minute by minute;
A horse-hoof slides on the brim,
And a horse plashes within it;
The long-legged moor-hens dive,
And hens to moor-cocks call;
Minute by minute they live:
The stone's in the midst of all.

Too long a sacrifice
Can make a stone of the heart.
O when may it suffice?
That is Heaven's part, our part
To murmur name upon name,
As a mother names her child
When sleep at last has come
On limbs that had run wild.
What is it but nightfall?
No, no, not night but death;
Was it needless death after all?
For England may keep faith
For all that is done and said.
We know their dream; enough
To know they dreamed and are dead;
And what if excess of love
Bewildered them till they died?
I write it out in a verse –
MacDonagh and MacBride

And Connolly and Pearse
Now and in time to be,
Wherever green is worn,
Are changed, changed utterly:
A terrible beauty is born.

W. B. Yeats (1865–1939)

The Wild Swans at Coole

THE trees are in their autumn beauty,
The woodland paths are dry,
Under the October twilight the water
Mirrors a still sky;
Upon the brimming water among the stones
Are nine-and-fifty Swans.

The nineteenth autumn has come upon me
Since I first made my count;
I saw, before I had well finished,
All suddenly mount
And scatter wheeling in great broken rings
Upon their clamorous wings.

I have looked upon those brilliant creatures,
And now my heart is sore.
All's changed since I, hearing at twilight,

The first time on this shore,
The bell-beat of their wings above my head,
Trod with a lighter tread.
Unwearied still, lover by lover,
They paddle in the cold
Companionable streams or climb the air;
Their hearts have not grown old;
Passion or conquest, wander where they will,
Attend upon them still.
But now they drift on the still water,
Mysterious, beautiful;
Among what rushes will they build,
By what lake's edge or pool
Delight men's eyes when I awake some day
To find they have flown away?

W. B. Yeats (1865–1939)

The Fiddler of Dooney

WHEN I play on my fiddle in Dooney,
Folk dance like a wave of the sea;
My cousin is priest in Kilcarnet,
My brother in Mocharabuiee.
I passed my brother and cousin:
They read in their books of prayer;
I read in my book of songs
I bought at the Sligo fair.
When we come at the end of time
To Peter sitting in state,
He will smile on the three old spirits,
But call me first through the gate;
For the good are always the merry,
Save by an evil chance,
And the merry love the fiddle,
And the merry love to dance:
And when the folk there spy me,
They will all come up to me,

With 'Here is the fiddler of Dooney!'
And dance like a wave of the sea.

W. B. Yeats (1865–1939)

The Lake Isle of Innisfree

I WILL arise and go now, and go to Innisfree,
And a small cabin build there, of clay and wattles made:
Nine bean-rows will I have there, a hive for the
   honey-bee,
And live alone in the bee-loud glade.
And I shall have some peace there, for peace comes
   dropping slow,
Dropping from the veils of the morning to where the
   cricket sings;
There midnight's all a glimmer, and noon a purple
   glow,
And evening full of the linnet's wings.

I will arise and go now, for always night and day
I hear lake water lapping with low sounds by the shore;
While I stand on the roadway, or on the pavements grey,
I hear it in the deep heart's core.

W. B. Yeats (1865–1939)

When You Are Old

WHEN you are old and grey and full of sleep,
And nodding by the fire, take down this book,
And slowly read, and dream of the soft look
Your eyes had once, and of their shadows deep;

How many loved your moments of glad grace,
And loved your beauty with love false or true,
But one man loved the pilgrim soul in you,
And loved the sorrows of your changing face;

And bending down beside the glowing bars,
Murmur, a little sadly, how Love fled
And paced upon the mountains overhead
And hid his face amid a crowd of stars.

W. B. Yeats (1865–1939)

He Wishes for the Cloths of Heaven

HAD I the heavens' embroidered cloths,
Enwrought with golden and silver light,
The blue and the dim and the dark cloths
Of night and light and the half-light;
I would spread the cloths under your feet:
But I, being poor, have only my dreams;
I have spread my dreams under your feet;
Tread softly because you tread on my dreams.

W. B. Yeats (1865–1939)

Age and Youth

WE have left our youth behind:
Earth is in its baby years:
Void of wisdom cries the wind,
And the sunlight knows no tears.

When shall twilight feel the awe,
All the rapt thought of the sage,
And the lips of wind give law
Drawn from out their lore of age?

When shall earth begin to burn
With such love as thrills my breast?
When shall we together turn
To our long, long home for rest?

Child and father, we grow old
While you laugh and play with flowers;
And life's tale for us is told
Holding only empty hours.

Giant child, on you await
All the hopes and fears of men.
In thy fullness is our fate –
What till then, oh, what till then?

George William Russell (AE) (1867–1935)

A Memory

You remember, dear, together
Two children, you and I,
Sat once in the autumn weather,
Watching the autumn sky.

There was some one round us straying
The whole of the long day through,
Who seemed to say, 'I am playing
At hide and seek with you.'

And one thing after another
Was whispered out of the air,
How God was a big, kind brother
Whose home is in everywhere.

His light like a smile comes glancing
Through the cool, cool winds as they pass,
From the flowers in heaven dancing
To the stars that shine in the grass.

- A MEMORY -

From the clouds in deep blue wreathing
And most from the mountains tall,
But God like a wind goes breathing
A dream of Himself in all.

The heart of the Wise was beating
Sweet, sweet, in our hearts that day:
And many a thought came fleeting
And fancies solemn and gay.

We were grave in our way divining
How childhood was taking wings,
And the wonder world was shining
With vast eternal things.

The solemn twilight fluttered
Like the plumes of seraphim,
And we felt what things were uttered
In the sunset voice of Him.

- A Memory -

We lingered long, for dearer
Than home were the mountain places
Where God from the stars dropt nearer
Our pale, dreamy faces.

Our very hearts from beating
We stilled in awed delight,
For spirit and children were meeting
In the purple, ample night.

George William Russell (AE) (1867–1935)

The Night Hunt

In the morning, in the dark
When the stars begin to blunt
By the walls of Barna Park
Dogs I heard and saw them hunt.
All the parish dogs were there,
All the dogs for miles around,
Teeming up behind a hare,
In the dark, without a sound.

How I heard I scarce can tell –
'Twas a patter in the grass –
And I did not see them well
Come across the dark and pass;
Yet I saw them and I knew
Spearman's dog and Spellman's dog
And, beside my own dog too,
Leamy's from the Island Bog.

In the morning when the sun
Burnished all the green to gorse,
I went out to take a run
Round the bog upon my horse;
And my dog that had been sleeping
In the heat beside the door
Left his yawning and went leaping
On a hundred yards before.

Through the village street we passed –
Not a dog there raised a snout –
Through the street and out at last
On the white bog road and out
Over Barna Park full pace,
Over to the Silver Stream,
Horse and dog in happy race,
Rider between thought and dream.

By the stream, at Leamy's house,
Lay a dog – my pace I curbed –
But our coming did not rouse
Him from drowsing undisturbed;
And my dog, as unaware
Of the other, dropped beside
And went running by me there
With my horse's slackened stride.

Yet by something, by a twitch
Of the sleeper's eye, a look
From the runner, something which
Little chords of feeling shook,
I was conscious that a thought
Shuddered through the silent deep
Of a secret – I had caught
Something I had known in sleep.

Thomas MacDonagh (1878–1916)

After a Year

AFTER a year of love
Death of love in a day;
And I who ever strove
To hold love in sure life
Now let it pass away
With no grief and no strife.

Pass – but it holds me yet;
Love, it would seem, may die;
But we cannot forget
And cannot be the same,
As lowly or as high,
As once, before this came.

Never as in old days
Can I again stoop low;
Never, now fallen, raise
Spirit and heart above
To where once life did show
The lone soul of my love.

None would the service ask
That she from love requires,
Making it not a task
But a high sacrament
Of all love's dear desires
And all life's grave intent.

And if she asked it not? –
Should I have loved her then? –
Such love was our one lot
And our true destiny.
Shall I find truth again? –
None could have known but she.

And she? – But it is vain
Her life now to surmise,
Whether of joy or pain,
After this borrowed year.
Memory may bring her sighs,
But will it bring a tear?

What if it brought love back? –
Love? – Ah! love died to-day –
She knew that our hearts lack
One thing that makes love true.
And I would not gainsay,
Told her I also knew.

And there an end of it–
I, who had never brooked
Such word as all unfit
For our sure love, brooked this –
Into her eyes I looked,
Left her without a kiss.

Thomas MacDonagh (1878–1916)

The Man Upright

I ONCE spent an evening in a village
Where the people are all taken up with tillage,
Or do some business in a small way
Among themselves, and all the day
Go crooked, doubled to half their size,
Both working and loafing, with their eyes
Stuck in the ground or in a board, –
For some of them tailor, and some of them hoard
Pence in a till in their little shops,
And some of them shoe-soles – they get the tops
Ready-made from England, and they die cobblers –
All bent up double, a village of hobblers
And slouchers and squatters, whether they struggle
Up and down, or bend to haggle
Over a counter, or bend at a plough,
Or to dig with a spade, or to milk a cow,
Or to shove the goose-iron stiffly along
The stuff on the sleeve-board, or lace the fong
In the boot on the last, or to draw the wax-end

Tight cross-ways – and so to make or to mend
What will soon be worn out by the crooked people.
The only thing straight in the place was the steeple,
I thought at first. I was wrong in that;
For there past the window at which I sat
Watching the crooked little men
Go slouching, and with the gait of a hen
An odd little woman go pattering past,
And the cobbler crouching over his last
In the window opposite, and next door
The tailor squatting inside on the floor –
While I watched them, as I have said before,
And thought that only the steeple was straight,
There came a man of a different gait –
A man who neither slouched nor pattered,
But planted his steps as if each step mattered;
Yet walked down the middle of the street
Not like a policeman on his beat,
But like a man with nothing to do
Except walk straight upright like me and you.

Thomas MacDonagh (1878–1916)

Lament for Thomas MacDonagh

HE shall not hear the bittern cry
In the wild sky, where he is lain,
Nor voices of the sweeter birds,
Above the wailing of the rain.

Nor shall he know when loud March blows
Thro' slanting snows her fanfare shrill,
Blowing to flame the golden cup
Of many an upset daffodil.

But when the Dark Cow leaves the moor
And pastures poor with greedy weeds
Perhaps he'll hear her low at morn
Lifting her horn in pleasant meads.

Francis Ledwidge (1887–1917)

Behind the Closed Eye

I walk the old frequented ways
That wind around the tangled braes,
I live again the sunny days
Ere I the city knew.

And scenes of old again are born,
The woodbine lassoing the thorn,
And drooping Ruth-like in the corn
The poppies weep the dew.

Above me in their hundred schools
The magpies bend their young to rules,
And like an apron full of jewels
The dewy cobweb swings.

And frisking in the stream below
The troutlets make the circles flow,

And the hungry crane doth watch them grow
As a smoker does his rings.

Above me smokes the little town,
With its whitewashed walls and roofs of brown
And its octagon spire toned smoothly down
As the holy minds within.

And wondrous impudently sweet,
Half of him passion, half conceit,
The blackbird calls adown the street
Like the piper of Hamelin.

I hear him, and I feel the lure
Drawing me back to the homely moor,
I'll go and close the mountain's door
On the city's strife and din.

Francis Ledwidge (1887–1917)

Ireland

I CALLED you by sweet names by wood and linn,
You answered not because my voice was new,
And you were listening for the hounds of Finn
And the long hosts of Lugh.

And so, I came unto a windy height
And cried my sorrow, but you heard no wind,
For you were listening to small ships in flight,
And the wail on hills behind.

And then I left you, wandering the war
Armed with will, from distant goal to goal,
To find you at the last free as of yore,
Or die to save your soul.

And then you called to us from far and near
To bring your crown from out the deeps of time,
It is my grief your voice I couldn't hear
In such a distant clime.

Francis Ledwidge (1887–1917)

To My Daughter Betty

In wiser days, my darling rosebud, blown
To beauty proud as was your Mother's prime.
In that desired, delayed, incredible time,
You'll ask why I abandoned you, my own,
And the dear heart that was your baby throne,
To die with death. And oh! they'll give you rhyme
And reason: some will call the thing sublime,
And some decry it in a knowing tone.
So here, while the mad guns curse overhead,
And tired men sigh with mud for couch and floor,
Know that we fools, now with the foolish dead,
Died not for flag, nor King, nor Emperor,
But for a dream, born in a herdsmen's shed,
And for the secret Scripture of the poor.

Thomas Kettle (1880–1916)

The Fairies

Up the airy mountain,
Down the rushy glen,
We daren't go a-hunting
For fear of little men;
Wee folk, good folk,
Trooping all together;
Green jacket, red cap,
And white owl's feather!

Down along the rocky shore
Some make their home,
They live on crispy pancakes
Of yellow tide-foam;
Some in the reeds
Of the black mountain lake,
With frogs for their watch-dogs,
All night awake.

High on the hill-top
The old King sits;
He is now so old and gray
He's nigh lost his wits.
With a bridge of white mist
Columbkill he crosses,
On his stately journeys
From Slieveleague to Rosses;
Or going up with music
On cold starry nights
To sup with the Queen
Of the gay Northern Lights.

They stole little Bridget
For seven years long;
When she came down again
Her friends were all gone.
They took her lightly back,
Between the night and morrow,

They thought that she was fast asleep,
But she was dead with sorrow.
They have kept her ever since
Deep within the lake,
On a bed of flag-leaves,
Watching till she wake.

By the craggy hill-side,
Through the mosses bare,
They have planted thorn-trees
For pleasure here and there.
If any man so daring
As dig them up in spite,
He shall find their sharpest thorns
In his bed at night.

Up the airy mountain,
Down the rushy glen,
We daren't go a-hunting

For fear of little men;
Wee folk, good folk,
Trooping all together;
Green jacket, red cap,
And white owl's feather!

William Allingham (1824–1889)

A Dream

I HEARD the dogs howl in the moonlight night;
I went to the window to see the sight;
All the Dead that I ever knew
Going one by one and two by two.

On they pass'd, and on they pass'd;
Townsfellows all, from first to last;
Born in the moonlight of the lane,
Quench'd in the heavy shadow again.

Schoolmates, marching as when they play'd
At soldiers once – but now more staid;
Those were the strangest sight to me
Who were drown'd, I knew, in the awful sea.

- A Dream -

Straight and handsome folk, bent and weak, too;
Some that I loved, and gasp'd to speak to;
Some but a day in their churchyard bed;
Some that I had not known were dead.

A long, long crowd – where each seem'd lonely,
Yet of them all there was one, one only,
Raised a head or look'd my way;
She linger'd a moment – she might not stay.

How long since I saw that fair pale face!
Ah! Mother dear! might I only place
My head on thy breast, a moment to rest,
While thy hand on my tearful cheek were prest!

- A Dream -

On, on, a moving bridge they made
Across the moon-stream, from shade to shade,
Young and old, women and men;
Many long-forgot, but remembered then,

And first there came a bitter laughter;
A sound of tears a moment after;
And then a music so lofty and gay,
That eve morning, day by day,
I strive to recall it if I may.

William Allingham (1824–1889)

The Mother

I DO not grudge them: Lord, I do not grudge
My two strong sons that I have seen go out
To break their strength and die, they and a few,
In bloody protest for a glorious thing.
They shall be spoken of among their people,
The generations shall remember them,
And call them blessed;
But I will speak their names to my own heart
In the long nights;
The little names that were familiar once
Round my dead hearth.

Lord, thou art hard on mothers:
We suffer in their coming and their going;
And tho' I grudge them not, I weary, weary
Of the long sorrow – And yet I have my joy:
My sons were faithful, and they fought.

Patrick H. Pearse (1879–1916)

The Wayfarer

THE beauty of the world hath made me sad,
This beauty that will pass;
Sometimes my heart hath shaken with great joy
To see a leaping squirrel in a tree,
Or a red lady-bird upon a stalk,
Or little rabbits in a field at evening,
Lit by a slanting sun,
Or some green hill where shadows drifted by,
Some quiet hill where mountainy man hath sown
And soon would reap; near to the gate of Heaven;

Or children with bare feet upon the sands
Of some ebbed sea, or playing on the streets
Of little towns in Connacht,
Things young and happy.
And then my heart hath told me:
These will pass,
Will pass and change, will die and be no more,
Things bright and green, things young and happy;
And I have gone upon my way,
Sorrowful.

Patrick H. Pearse (1879–1916)

The Fool

SINCE the wise men have not spoken, I speak that am
  only a fool;
A fool that hath loved his folly,
Yea, more than the wise men their books or their
  counting houses or their quiet homes,
Or their fame in men's mouths;
A fool that in all his days hath done never a
  prudent thing,
Never hath counted the cost, nor recked if
  another reaped
The fruit of his mighty sowing, content to scatter
  the seed;
A fool that is unrepentant, and that soon at the end of all
Shall laugh in his lonely heart as the ripe ears fall to the
  reaping-hooks
And the poor are filled that were empty,
Tho' he go hungry.
I have squandered the splendid years that the Lord God
  gave to my youth

In attempting impossible things, deeming them alone
   worth the toil.

Was it folly or grace? Not men shall judge me, but God.
I have squandered the splendid years:
Lord, if I had the years I would squander them
   over again,
Aye, fling them from me!
For this I have heard in my heart, that a man shall
   scatter, not hoard,
Shall do the deed of to-day, nor take thought of
   tomorrow's teen,
Shall not bargain or huxter with God; or was it a jest
   of Christ's
And is this my sin before men, to have taken Him at
   His word?
The lawyers have sat in council, the men with the keen,
   long faces,
And said, 'This man is a fool,' and others have said,

'He blasphemeth';
And the wise have pitied the fool that hath striven to
  give a life
In the world of time and space among the bulks of
  actual things,
To a dream that was dreamed in the heart, and that only
  the heart could hold.

O wise men, riddle me this: what if the dream
  come true?
What if the dream come true? and if millions unborn
  shall dwell
In the house that I shaped in my heart, the noble house
  of my thought?
Lord, I have staked my soul, I have staked the lives of
  my kin
On the truth of Thy dreadful word. Do not remember
  my failures,
But remember this my faith

And so I speak.
Yea, ere my hot youth pass, I speak to my people and say:
Ye shall be foolish as I; ye shall scatter, not save:
Ye shall venture your all, lest ye lose what is more
than all;
Ye shall call for a miracle, taking Christ at His word.
And for this I will answer, O people, answer here
and hereafter,
O people that I have loved, shall we not answer together?

Patrick H. Pearse (1879–1916)

No Song

I LOOSE the secrets of my soul
And mint my heart to heavy words
Lest you should need to ask a dole
Of singing from the winds and birds –
You will not heed nor bear my soul.

I coin again a greater sum
Of silence, and you will not heed:
The fallow spaces call you 'Come,
The season's ripe to sow the seed' –
Both I and these are better dumb.

I have no way to make you hear,
No song will echo in your heart;
Now must I with the fading year
Fade.
Without meeting we must part –
No song nor silence you will hear.

Joseph Mary Plunkett (1887–1916)

A Wave of the Sea

I AM a wave of the sea
And the foam of the wave
And the wind of the foam
And the wings of the wind.

My soul's in the salt of the sea
In the weight of the wave
In the bubbles of foam
In the ways of the wind.

My gift is the depth of the sea
The strength of the wave
The lightness of foam
The speed of the wind.

Joseph Mary Plunkett (1887–1916)

I See His Blood Upon the Rose

I SEE his blood upon the rose
And in the stars the glory of his eyes,
His body gleams amid eternal snows,
His tears fall from the skies.

I see his face in every flower;
The thunder and the singing of the birds
Are but his voice – and carven by his power
Rocks are his written words.

All pathways by his feet are worn,
His strong heart stirs the ever-beating sea,
His crown of thorns is twined with every thorn,
His cross is every tree.

Joseph Mary Plunkett (1887–1916)

In the Wilderness

GAUNT windy moons bedraggled in the dusk
Have drifted by and withered in their shame,
The once-proud Thunder-Terror, fallen tame,
Noses for truffles with unwhetted tusk;
A sickening scent of civet and of musk
Has clogged the nostrils of the Hound of Fame –
But flickering stars are blown to vivid flame
When leaps your beauty from its blazing husk.

Blossom of burning solitude! High things
Are lit with splendour – Love your glimmering ray
Smites them to glory – below them and away
A little song floats upward on the wings
Of daring, and the thunders of the Day
Clamour to God the messages it brings.

Joseph Mary Plunkett (1887–1916)

Dear Heart, Why Will You Use Me So?

DEAR heart, why will you use me so?
Dear eyes that gently me upbraid,
Still are you beautiful – but O,
How is your beauty raimented!

Through the clear mirror of your eyes,
Through the soft sigh of kiss to kiss,
Desolate winds assail with cries
The shadowy garden where love is.

And soon shall love dissolved be
When over us the wild winds blow –
But you, dear love, too dear to me,
Alas! why will you use me so?

James Joyce (1882–1941)

Gentle Lady, Do Not Sing

GENTLE lady, do not sing
Sad songs about the end of love;
Lay aside sadness and sing
How love that passes is enough.

Sing about the long deep sleep
Of lovers that are dead, and how
In the grave all love shall sleep:
Love is aweary now.

James Joyce (1882–1941)

I Hear an Army Charging Upon the Land

I HEAR an army charging upon the land,
And the thunder of horses plunging, foam about their
   knees:
Arrogant, in black armour, behind them stand,
Disdaining the reins, with fluttering whips, the
   charioteers.

They cry unto the night their battle-name:
I moan in sleep when I hear afar their whirling laughter.
They cleave the gloom of dreams, a binding flame,
Clanging, clanging upon the heart as upon an anvil.

They come shaking in triumph their long green hair:
They come out of the sea and run shouting by the shore.
My heart, have you no wisdom this to despair?
My love, my love, why have you left me alone?

James Joyce (1882–1941)

She Weeps Over Rahoon

RAIN on Rahoon falls softly, softly falling,
Where my dark lover lies.
Sad is his voice that calls me, sadly calling,
At grey moonrise.

Love, hear thou
How soft, how sad his voice is ever calling,
Ever unanswered, and the dark rain falling,
Then as now.

Dark too our hearts, O love, shall lie and cold
As his sad heart has lain
Under the moongrey nettles, the black mould
And muttering rain.

James Joyce (1882–1941)

Father and Son

ONLY last week, watching the hushed fields
Of our moist lovely Meath, now thinned by November,
I came to where the road from Laracor leads
To the Boyne river – that seems more lake than river,
Stretched in uneasy light and stript of weeds.

And walking longside an old weir
Of my people's, where nothing stirs – only the shadowed
Leaden flight of a heron up the lean air –
I went unmanly with grief, knowing how my father,
Happy though captive in years, walked last with me
there.

Yes, happy in Meath with me for a day
He walked, taking stock of herds hid in their own
breathing;
And naming colts, gusty as wind, once steered by his
hand,

Lightnings winked in the eyes that were half shy in
   greeting
Old friends – the wild blades, when he gallivanted the
   land.

For that proud, wayward man now my heart breaks –
Breaks for that man whose mind was a secret eyrie,
Whose kind hand was sole signet of his race,
Who curbed me, scorned my green ways, yet increasingly
   loved me
Till Death drew its grey blind down his face.

And yet I am pleased that even my reckless ways
Are living shades of his rich calms and passions –
Witnesses for him and for those faint namesakes
With whom now he is one, under yew branches,
Yes, one in a graven silence no bird breaks.

Frederick Robert Higgins (1896–1941)

Padraic Ó Conaire, Gaelic Storyteller

THEY'VE paid the last respects in sad tobacco
And silent is this wakehouse in its haze;
They've paid the last respects; and now their whiskey
Flings laughing words on mouths of prayer and praise;
And so young couples huddle by the gables.
O let them grope home through the hedgy night –
Alone I'll mourn my old friend, while the cold dawn
Thins out the holy candlelight.

Respects are paid to one loved by the people
Ah, was he not – among our mighty poor –
The sudden wealth cast on those pools of darkness,
Those bearing, just, a star's faint signature;
And so he was to me, close friend, near brother,
Dear Padraic of the wide and sea-cold eyes –
So lovable, so courteous and noble,
The very west was in his soft replies.

They'll miss his heavy stick and stride in Wicklow –
His story-talking down Winetavern Street,
Where old men sitting in the wizen daylight
Have kept an edge upon his gentle wit;
While women on the grassy streets of Galway,
Who hearken for his passing – but in vain,
Shall hardly tell his step as shadows vanish
Through archways of forgotten Spain.

Ah, they'll say, Padraic's gone again exploring;
But now down glens of brightness, O he'll find
An alehouse overflowing with wise Gaelic
That's braced in vigour by the bardic mind,
And there his thoughts shall find their own forefathers –
In minds to whom our heights of race belong,
In crafty men, who ribbed a ship or turned
The secret joinery of song.

Alas, death mars the parchment of his forehead;
And yet for him, I know, the earth is mild –
The windy fidgets of September grasses
Can never tease a mind that loved the wild;
So drink his peace – this grey juice of the barley
Runs with a light that ever pleased his eye –
While old flames nod and gossip on the hearthstone
And only the young winds cry.

Frederick Robert Higgins (1896–1941)

I Am the Mountainy Singer

I AM the mountainy singer –
The voice of the peasant's dream,
The cry of the wind on the wooded hill,
The leap of the fish in the stream.

Quiet and love I sing –
The carn on the mountain crest,
The cailín in her lover's arms,
The child at its mother's breast.

Beauty and peace I sing –
The fire on the open hearth,
The cailleach spinning at her wheel,
The plough in the broken earth.

Travail and pain I sing –
The bride on the childing bed,
The dark man labouring at his rhymes,
The ewe in the lambing shed.

Sorrow and death I sing –
The canker come on the corn,
The fisher lost in the mountain loch,
The cry at the mouth of morn.

No other life I sing,
For I am sprung of the stock
That broke the hilly land for bread,
And built the nest in the rock!

Joseph Campbell (1879–1944)

The Old Woman

As a white candle
In a holy place,
So is the beauty
Of an aged face.

As the spent radiance
Of the winter sun,
So is a woman
With her travail done.

Her brood gone from her,
And her thoughts as still
As the waters
Under a ruined mill.

Joseph Campbell (1879–1944)

The Planter's Daughter

WHEN night stirred at sea
And the fire brought a crowd in
They say that her beauty
Was music in mouth
And few in the candlelight
Thought her too proud,
For the house of the planter
Is known by the trees.

Men that had seen her
Drank deep and were silent,
The women were speaking
Wherever she went –
As a bell that is rung
Or a wonder told shyly,
And O she was the Sunday
In every week.

Austin Clarke (1896–1974)

The Poet

'THE blackbird's on the briar
The seagull's on the ground –
They are nests, and they're more than nests,' he said,
'They are tokens I have found.

There, where the rain-dashed briar
Marks an empty glade,
The blackbird's nest is seen,' he said,
'Clay-rimmed, uncunningly made.

By shore of the inland lake,
Where surgeless water shoves,
The seagulls have their nests,' he said,
'As low as cattles' hooves.'

I heard a poet say it,
The sojourner of a night;
His head was up to the rafter
Where he stood in candles' light.

'Your houses are like the seagulls'
Nests – they are scattered and low;
Like the blackbirds' nests in briars,' he said,
'Uncunningly made – even so:

But close to the ground are reared
The wings that have widest sway,
And the birds that sing best in the wood,' he said,
'Were reared with breasts to the clay.

You've wildness – I've turned it to song;
You've strength – I've turned it to wings;
The welkin's for your conquest then,
The wood to your music rings.'

I heard a poet say it,
The sojourner of a night;
His head was up to the rafter
Where he stood in candles' light.

Padraic Colum (1881–1972)

To Be Dead

To be dead is to stop believing in
The masterpieces we will begin tomorrow;
To be an exile is to be a coward,
To know that growth has stopped.
That whatever is done is the end;
Correct the proofs over and over,
Rewrite old poems again and again,
Tell lies to yourself about your achievement:
Ten printed books on the shelves.
Though you know that no one loves you for
What you have done,
But for what you might do.

And you perhaps take up religion bitterly
Which you laughed at in your youth,
Well not actually laughed
But it wasn't your kind of truth.

Patrick Kavanagh (1904–1967)

Epic

I HAVE lived in important places, times
When great events were decided, who owned
That half a rood of rock, a no-man's land
Surrounded by our pitchfork-armed claims.
I heard the Duffys shouting 'Damn your soul'
And old McCabe stripped to the waist, seen
Step the plot defying blue-cast-steel –
'Here is the march along these iron stones.'
That was the year of the Munich bother. Which
Was most important? I inclined
To lose my faith in Ballyrush and Gortin
Till Homer's ghost came whispering to my mind.
He said: I made the Iliad from such
A local row. Gods make their own importance.

Patrick Kavanagh (1904–1967)

No Music

I'll tell you a sore truth, little understood
It's harder to leave, than to be left:
To stay, to leave, both sting wrong.

You will always have me to blame,
Can dream we might have sailed on;
From absence's rib, a warm fiction.

To tear up old love by the roots,
To trample on past affections:
There is no music for so harsh a song.

John Montague (born 1929)

Follower

My father worked with a horse-plough,
His shoulders globed like a full sail strung
Between the shafts and the furrow,
The horse strained at his clicking tongue.

An expert. He would set the wing
And fit the bright steel-pointed sock.
The sod rolled over without breaking.
At the head-rig, with a single pluck

Of reins, the sweating team turned round
And back into the land. His eye
Narrowed and angled at the ground,
Mapping the furrow exactly.

I stumbled in his hob-nailed wake
Fell sometimes on the polished sod;
Sometimes he rode me on his back
Dipping and rising to his plod.

I wanted to grow up and plough,
To close one eye, stiffen my arm.
All I ever did was follow
In his broad shadow round the farm.

I was a nuisance, tripping, falling,
Yapping always. But today
It is my father who keeps stumbling
Behind me, and will not go away.

Seamus Heaney (1939–2013)

Postscript

AND some time make the time to drive out west
Into County Clare, along the Flaggy Shore,
In September or October, when the wind
And the light are working off each other
So that the ocean on one side is wild
With foam and glitter, and inland among stones
The surface of a slate-grey lake is lit
By the earthed lightning of a flock of swans,
Their feathers roughed and ruffling, white on white,
Their fully-grown headstrong-looking heads
Tucked or cresting or busy underwater.
Useless to think you'll park and capture it
More thoroughly. You are neither here nor there,
A hurry through which known and strange things pass
As big soft buffetings come at the car sideways
And catch the heart off guard and blow it open.

Seamus Heaney (1939–2013)

Mid-Term Break

I SAT all morning in the college sick bay
Counting bells knelling classes to a close.
At two o'clock our neighbours drove me home.

In the porch I met my father crying –
He had always taken funerals in his stride –
And Big Jim Evans saying it was a hard blow.

The baby cooed and laughed and rocked the pram
When I came in, and I was embarrassed
By old men standing up to shake my hand

And tell me they were 'sorry for my trouble,'
Whispers informed strangers I was the eldest,
Away at school, as my mother held my hand

In hers and coughed out angry tearless sighs.
At ten o'clock the ambulance arrived
With the corpse, stanched and bandaged by the nurses.

Next morning I went up into the room. Snowdrops
And candles soothed the bedside; I saw him
For the first time in six weeks. Paler now,

Wearing a poppy bruise on his left temple,
He lay in the four foot box as in his cot.
No gaudy scars, the bumper knocked him clear.

A four foot box, a foot for every year.

Seamus Heaney (1939–2013)

From the Painting *Back from Market* by Chardin

DRESSED in the colours of a country day –
Grey-blue, blue-grey, the white of seagulls' bodies –
Chardin's peasant woman
Is to be found at all times in her short delay
Of dreams, her eyes mixed
Between love and market, empty flagons of wine
At her feet, bread under her arm. He has fixed
Her limbs in colour and her heart in line.

In her right hand the hindlegs of a hare
Peep from a cloth sack. Through the door
Another woman moves
In painted daylight. Nothing in this bare
Closet has been lost
Or changed. I think of what great art removes:
Hazard and death. The future and the past.
A woman's secret history and her loves –

And even the dawn market from whose bargaining
She has just come back, where men and women
Congregate and go
Among the produce, learning to live from morning
To next day, linked
By a common impulse to survive, although
In surging light they are single and distinct
Like birds in the accumulating snow.

Eavan Boland (born 1944)

Old Cuillonaghtan

Up on top of the hill here, all forgotten,
Is the village without its people,
Without its children's songs in the halflight
Between the gables. And the lulling beauty
Of the lullabies are no longer soft in the mothers'
Mouths. How I would love to pass here
One evening, when the swifts are dipping as now
To the wet tufts, and suddenly see the villagers
Returned, the broken cooking-pots
Carried back whole into the frosty kitchens
And set again to be fathered by the low flames

Of the fires that never went out – the blowing turf,
A few smoking sods on a spade, carried
Down to a hearth in the lower village
When the last of the people went away,
The happiness and the history harboured there
For the time the people would come back.
They never did. Their descendants maybe
Have forgotten Cuillonaghtan, where the heather
Faithfully fumes with purple every chilly March,
To be seen by nobody of any consequence.
I have only the curiosity of a stranger.

Sebastian Barry (born 1955)

Biographies

Allingham, William (1824–1889)

Born in Ballyshannon, County Donegal, son of a bank manager of English descent, he worked as a customs official until 1870, then devoted himself exclusively to writing.

Barry, Sebastian (born 1955)

The award-winning Dublin-born novelist and playwright began his literary career as a poet. His poetry collections include *The Water-Colourist* (1983) and *Fanny Hawke Goes to the Mainland Forever* (1989).

Boland, Eavan (born 1944)

The Dublin-born poet writes about women's experience of life in Ireland. A prolific and award-winning poet, she has also been a teacher of literature at third level in Ireland and the US.

Campbell, Joseph (1879–1944)

Belfast-born Campbell is best known as the lyricist who supplied the words to many traditional airs, including 'My Lagan Love'. He supported the 1916 Rising and was interned during the Civil War.

Clarke, Austin (1896–1974)

The Dublin-born journalist, poet and playwright wrote 18 books of verse, the first published in 1917. His novel *The Bright Temptation* (1932) was banned in Ireland until 1954.

Colum, Padraic (1881–1972)

Colum was born in County Longford, moving to Dublin in 1892. A member of the Gaelic League, he was on the first board of the Abbey Theatre. Poet, novelist, playwright and biographer, he had a particular interest in Irish folklore.

Davis, Thomas (1814–1845)

Davis was born in Mallow, County Cork. He devoted his life to the cause of Irish nationalism, as his poetry reflects. Together with Charles Gavan Duffy and John Blake Dillon he founded *The Nation* newspaper.

De Vere, Aubrey (1814–1902)

Born in Limerick to a titled family, this prolific poet and critic was a recognised disciple of Wordsworth. He was a fervent supporter of the Celtic revival.

Drennan, William (1754–1820)

Son of a Belfast clergyman, Drennan was a physician, an early advocate of smallpox inoculation. A co-founder of the United

Irishmen, he wrote many of the organisation's pamphlets, and is credited with coining the phrase 'the emerald isle'.

Dubois, Dorothea (1728–1774)

Eldest daughter of the heir to the earldom of Anglesey, Dubois was declared illegitimate when her father repudiated his marriage to her mother. Cast into poverty, she took to writing, famously telling the story of her father's actions in *Poems by a Lady of Quality* (1764).

Emmet, Robert (1778–1803)

Son of a middle-class Dublin family, Emmet became interested in nationalist politics while studying at Trinity College. He was involved in the failed rebellion of 1798. Arrested in the aftermath of another unsuccessful rising in 1803, he was tried and executed for treason.

Ferguson, Samuel (1810–1886)

Widely regarded as a forerunner of the Irish literary revival, this Ulster-born barrister, writer and antiquarian studied at Trinity College Dublin. He was elected president of the Royal Irish Academy and held open house at his home in Howth for lovers of literature, art and music.

Heaney, Seamus (1939–2013)

Lauded as a literary giant of the twentieth century, the poet, playwright, translator, lecturer and Nobel laureate was born in County Derry, the eldest of nine children. His work is full of the small details that infuse everyday life.

Henry, James (1798–1876)

Born in Dublin, Henry was a physician, poet and classical scholar dedicated to the study of the works of Virgil. His self-published poetry received no critical acclaim in his lifetime, but eight of his poems were 'rediscovered' and reprinted in an anthology of Victorian verse in 1987.

Higgins, Frederick Robert (1896–1941)

Born in Foxford, County Mayo, Higgins was a poet and theatre director whose best-known work is a collection of poetry entitled *The Gap of Brightness*.

Joyce, James (1882–1941)

A colossus of the Irish and world literary scenes, Joyce was born and educated in Dublin, but emigrated to mainland Europe in his early twenties. Despite this, all his novels are set in Dublin. His most famous novel is *Ulysses*, and his most popular collection of poetry is *Pomes Penyeach*.

Edward A. McGuire *Seamus Heaney*

Kavanagh, Patrick (1904–1967)

Kavanagh was born in County Monaghan and spent 20 years farming before embarking on a literary career in Dublin. Long regarded as an outsider by the Dublin literary establishment, he built a reputation as a lyric poet. His novel *Tarry Flynn* (1948), was banned by the Irish censor.

Kettle, Thomas (1880–1916)

A Dublin-born barrister and writer and MP for East Tyrone from 1906–10. He enlisted at the outbreak of World War I and was killed in 1916 at the Battle of the Somme.

Ledwidge, Francis (1887–1917)

Born in Slane, County Meath, and largely self-educated, Ledwidge enlisted in Lord Dunsany's regiment in 1914 and was killed in action at the Battle of Passchendaele. Published during his lifetime and posthumously, he became known as the 'poet of the blackbirds'.

MacDonagh, Thomas (1878–1916)

An Irish poet and nationalist and friend of Patrick Pearse, MacDonagh taught at Pearse's school and founded the Association of Secondary Teachers in Ireland. A signatory to the Proclamation of the Republic, he was executed on 3 May 1916 as one of the leaders of the Easter Rising.

Malone, Carroll (182?–1892)

Carroll Malone is the *nom de plume* of William McBurney, a native of County Down who emigrated to Boston and wrote many pieces for *The Boston Pilot*. 'The Croppy Boy' was once sung at most Irish nationalist gatherings in the US.

Mangan, James Clarence (1803–1849)

Mangan was born in Dublin, the son of a former hedge school teacher. He taught himself German and did some work as a translator, later turning to writing poetry. After the Great Famine, his work became political in nature, displaying a strong nationalist fervour.

McCarroll, James (1814–1892)

Born in Longford, the young McCarroll emigrated to Ontario, Canada, in 1831. A harsh critic of the living conditions of Irish immigrants, he was also a staunch Irish nationalist, writing for the *Fenian Volunteer*. Branded a traitor in Canada, he moved to the US in the mid-1860s.

Montague, John (born 1929)

Montague was born in Brooklyn, New York. He returned to Ireland in 1933 and was first published while studying at University College Dublin. His award-winning work focuses on the themes of exile, loss and national identity.

Moore, Thomas (1779–1852)

The Dublin-born poet, singer and songwriter is best known for his lyrics to 'The Minstrel Boy' and 'The Last Rose of Summer'. A friend of Lord Byron's, he famously burned the poet's memoirs in order to protect his posthumous reputation.

O'Curry, Eugene (1794–1862)

The son of a Clare farmer, O'Curry spent some years as a travelling pedlar, and became interested in Irish music and folklore. A supporter of Catholic emancipation and a well-regarded historian, he was elected to the Royal Irish Academy in 1851.

O'Reilly, John Boyle (1844–1890)

Drogheda-born O'Reilly became involved in the Fenian movement and was sentenced to death for treason, but the sentence was commuted to transportation to Australia. He escaped to America, where he lived for the rest of his life.

Pearse, Patrick H. (1879–1916)

A teacher, barrister, writer, nationalist and political activist, he was one of the leaders of the Easter Rising and a signatory to the Proclamation. He was executed on 3 May 1916.

Plunkett, Joseph Mary (1887–1916)

An Irish poet and nationalist, many of whose poems have a

religious theme. As one of the planners of the 1916 Rising he was executed on 4 May 1916, just a few hours after marrying Grace Gifford in the chapel of Kilmainham Gaol.

Rolleston, T.W. (1857–1920)

The Trinity-educated son of a judge, Rolleston was involved in the Gaelic League. He worked as a journalist and civil servant and wrote on a wide range of subjects, but had a particular interest in Irish legends and mythology.

Russell, George William (1867–1935)

Born in Lurgan, County Armagh, this Irish nationalist, theosophist, critic, poet, novelist and painter wrote under the pseudonym 'AE'. He was a lifelong friend of W. B. Yeats.

Sheridan, Richard Brinsley (1751–1816)

A poet and playwright best known for his plays *The Rivals* (1775) and *A School for Scandal* (1777). An owner of the Drury Theatre, London, Sheridan was also involved in the stormy politics of the day. As a Whig MP he was outspoken in his support of the French Revolution.

Swift, Jonathan (1667–1745)

Anglican cleric, poet, satirist, pamphleteer, Jonathan Swift was dean of St Patrick's Cathedral, Dublin, and achieved worldwide renown with his novel *Gulliver's Travels*. His will established a hospital for the mentally ill in Dublin, St Patrick's, one of the first dedicated psychiatric hospitals in the world.

Synge, John Millington (1871–1909)

Synge was a dominant figure in the Irish literary revival and a founder of the Abbey Theatre. His plays, including *Riders to the Sea* (1904) and *The Playboy of the Western World* (1907), set the style of production at the Abbey for decades.

Tighe, Mary (1772–1810)

Tighe was born in Dublin, moving to London in 1793. In 1805 she published her allegorical poem 'Psyche'.

Todhunter, John (1839–1916)

Born in Dublin to a Quaker family, Todhunter studied medicine at Trinity College, also winning prizes for literature. He was a founder of the Irish Literary Society in London.

Tynan, Katharine (1861–1931)

Tynan was born in Dublin and is ranked among the poets of World War I. Two of her sons fought in the war, one in Palestine and one in France and much of her poetry is written from her experience as the mother of soldiers.

Wilde, Jane (1821–1896)

Lady Jane Wilde was a dedicated supporter of Irish nationalism, writing for, and subsequently editing *The Nation* under the pseudonym John Fanshaw Ellis. Her poetry, frequently written under the *nom de plume* 'Speranza', highlighted the plight of the Irish people.

Wilde, Oscar (1854–1900)

Dublin-born Wilde was notorious for his wit and charm. Renowned as a master of the epigram, he was a prolific poet and playwright and also wrote children's tales. His health suffered when he was imprisoned for offences against morality in 1895, and the only work he published after his release was 'The Ballad of Reading Gaol'.

Yeats, William Butler (1865–1939)

Son of the painter John B. Yeats, the poet and playwright was very involved with the Celtic revival, which influenced much of his work. In 1923 he was awarded the Nobel Prize for Literature and his poetry is acclaimed worldwide.

List of illustrations and picture credits